How to Raise Goldfish and Guppies

A Child's Book of Pet Care

by Sara Bonnett Stein
photographs by Robert Weinreb

Random House   **New York**

Created by The Open Family Press/Media Projects Incorporated. Design by Mary Gale Moyes.

The photographs of the newt, the tadpole, the water strider, and the turtle on page 45 are courtesy of Ray Gilbert and the New Canaan Nature Center, New Canaan, Connecticut.

Library of Congress Cataloging in Publication Data

Stein, Sara Bonnett. How to raise goldfish and guppies. (A Child's book of pet care) Includes index. SUMMARY: An easy-to-read guide to the care of goldfish and guppies, including discussions on selection, proper equipment, and fish physiology and behavior.   1. Goldfish—Juvenile literature.   2. Guppies—Juvenile literature.   3. Aquariums—Juvenile literature.   [1. Goldfish.   2. Guppies.   3. Aquariums]   I. Title. SF458.G6S74   639'.375'3   76-8139   ISBN 0-394-83225-6   ISBN 0-394-93225-0 lib. bdg.

Manufactured in the United States of America   1 2 3 4 5 6 7 8 9 0

Table of Contents

A Note to Parents

Few young children approach a pet fish as *just* a fish. They tend to view animals as creatures much like themselves. They assume a pet fish thinks as they do, feels the same emotions, and understands their language. They try to make friends. Many children try to befriend a fish as they would a kitten or a hamster: by talking and by touching. Of course that doesn't work with a fish. If your child expects a pet fish to be responsive, be prepared for possible disappointment before he or she learns to see the fish another way.

Some children make friends with a fish as they would with the inhabitants of a dollhouse: by gazing, by arranging, and by imagining. This approach works better. There are no expectations that can't be met. So this book gently tries to dissuade children from the first approach and encourage them toward the second. It also tries to help them see fish as they really are.

Parents have expectations, too. You may hope a pet fish will be an educational experience, or that the responsibility of caring for an animal will help your child grow. But if your child has not asked to have a fish, make it a family pet instead. Requiring a child to assume responsibility for a pet he never requested only leads to disappointment. The child finds the gift a burden. The parents are unhappy with their child's indifference. Indifference results in hasty handfuls of food, a dirty tank—and a dead fish.

But many children do love fish and beg to have one. They gaze into the tanks in stores as though they wanted to join the world on the other side of the glass. They tap. They are knocking to come in.

There are ways to enter that underwater world. One way is through understanding how fish live. Children notice a lot. So this book explains to your child what he or she is watching in an aquarium. Another way to enter a fish's world is by creating an underwater landscape and imagining what it would be like to live there. This book tells your child how to build an underwater world with plants, rocks, and sand.

Learning to appreciate a fish is easier than learning to take care of one. Who's going to clean the tank? A five-year-old can siphon a tank with help. A three-year-old can't. And since siphoning is at best a wet and clumsy job, even a ten-year-old can use a helping hand. Siphoning must be done every week. It takes half an hour. If siphoning causes family despair, installing a filter will be worth the money.

And who's going to feed the fish? That's easy. Children love to feed fish. But *remembering* to feed fish isn't easy at all. If your child is under eight, keep the tank in the kitchen or family room, or wherever you are all together once a day. Then someone can say, "Time to feed the fish."

This book includes all the practical information you and your child need to buy and raise healthy fish. The first chapter, "Buying Your Fish," describes the fish themselves and the necessary equipment. The varieties of goldfish suggested are the most vigorous ones. Fancier varieties, such as the delicate Lionheads and Celestials, die more easily. Common Guppies are the only guppy variety suggested. All the fancy hybrid guppies require a tropical tank setup with heater and thermostat. The cost of the recommended fish is minimal: guppies are about 25¢ each; baby goldfish about 50¢. The basic equipment—tank, siphon, net—comes to less than $11.00. A three-quarter-ounce can of high-quality, flake-type goldfish food costs 89¢ and lasts one goldfish two or three months. A one-ounce can of good guppy food costs $1.29 and lasts a pair of guppies two or three months. (Cheaper food is available, but it is not likely to be as nutritious as the more expensive brands.)

The second chapter, "Caring for Your Fish," has clearly illustrated instructions for feeding the fish and for siphoning the tank. It also explains how to set up a self-cleaning tank. The self-cleaning setup costs less than $10.00 for pump, filter, and a supply of charcoal and dacron filter fluff.

There may be a problem if you have a cat. Some cats live at peace with fish, but most can't resist the temptation to go fishing. The only solution is a special tank cover sold in pet stores and pet departments. A cover

4

to fit a five-and-a-half-gallon tank costs about $2.00. Since the cover cuts off fresh air, a filter and pump become a necessity. There are no covers made for fishbowls.

With proper feeding and a clean tank, pet guppies can live for several years, and pet goldfish for as long as 20 years. But even with the best of care, fish in tanks get sick easily. There are many medicines on the market, but few people can tell you what ails a sick fish. Both vets and pet dealers may be less helpful than a friend or neighbor who keeps tropical fish as a hobby. Because it is common for a child's fish to die, this chapter ends with a description of a burial. The suggestion to bury a dead fish may not seem practical when the toilet is so handy, but respect for life demands burial for even a guppy.

"Fish Watching," the next chapter, discusses fish behavior—how fish breathe and swim, what senses they have, why they act as they do. The wonder of guppy multiplication is also discussed, since a pair of guppies are sure to reproduce.

The book ends with "Underwater Worlds," which suggests innocent fantasies that will satisfy a child without harming his fish. The tank arrangement shown in the photographs was conceived and built by children. The six plants recommended are all hardy in an unheated tank. In combination, they provide bell-like flowers, waving grasses, staunch leaves. The cost of plants and accessories is often allowance-sized, or at least no strain on the budget. The exception is artificial lighting for plants, which may be needed to supplement natural light. A tank fixture that takes the trouble-free Gro-Lux fluorescent bulb costs $15.00 or more. The bulb itself costs $3.00.

There is no reason, however, to build a world in a weekend. Take your time. Find a pretty piece of quartz. Save glass jewels from dime-store finery. Try a pond plant. Make a clay castle. Catch a water bug. As your child's underwater world grows, so will his participation in it. And that's what pet fish are for.

Chapter One
Buying Your Fish

A fish is a different kind of pet. He is not like a hamster or a parakeet or a puppy. Those pets live in your world with you. You can touch them and be friends with them. But a fish does not live in your world. You must live on land with air all around you. A fish must live in a tank with water all around him. You can watch a fish go about his water life, but he is not interested in your land life.

Sometimes people become impatient when their fish does not seem to notice them. They want to make friends. They put their hand in the tank and try to touch his body. But the fish doesn't understand. He thinks that an enemy is after him. He is frightened and tries to get away.

Sometimes people tap on the side of the tank to get their fish to pay attention to them. The fish feels the shock of the tapping through the water. He acts upset, as though something had hit him. But he still does not pay attention to his owner. He doesn't even know that he has an owner.

You have to love a fish in a different way. You can love him by watching him and understanding his way of living. You can love him by feeding him and caring for him. And you can love him by making his water world beautiful.

When you love a fish this way, something good happens. Your mind moves into his world with him.

You can imagine how it feels to be a fish. You can almost feel the water smooth on your own skin. You can pretend you are swimming between waving grasses. You can picture finding a tiny shrimp for dinner and gulping it down.

A fish does not have any imagination. But you do. A fish can't share your world. But you can share his.

Getting Ready for Your Fish

The day before you buy a fish, you have to get water ready for his tank. Find a pot or a pail that holds five gallons of water. Wash the pail with salt, not with soap. Put the salt on a damp sponge and rub it around the pail. Rinse the pail out very well. Now fill the pail with water from the tap. Put the pail in the room where your fish will live. In a day, the water will be at the same temperature as the room. This is about the same temperature that the fish is used to in the pet store.

Unlike you, a fish can't control how warm or cold his body is. His body gets warm if the water is warm, and cool if the water is cool. If you put him into water that is warmer or cooler than he is used to, his body temperature changes too quickly. He gets sick or even dies.

As soon as the water is ready, you can go and buy your fish in a pet store or in the pet section of a department store. You can buy the equipment he needs at the same time. Get a tank or a wide-mouthed bowl, a siphon with a squeeze bulb for cleaning the tank or bowl, and a net for catching your fish. Also buy some fish food.

You might need a bottle of chlorine remover too. Many cities and towns have chlorine in their water. Chlorine is poison to fish. Ask the pet dealer about the water where you live. If he says you need chlorine remover, buy a bottle and follow the directions on it. Chlorine remover works right away, so you can add the right number of drops to the water just before you put your fish in his tank.

When you see pet fish in cartoons, they always seem to be in bowls. Fish look cute in round bowls. The trouble is, most fishbowls are not good for fish. Fish breathe air that is dissolved in water. As fish breathe, they use up the air. New air gets into the water at the top of the tank or bowl. Not enough air gets into bowls with small mouths.

Your fish needs a tank or a wide-mouthed bowl. These containers let enough air into the water. Your fish can breathe easily in them.

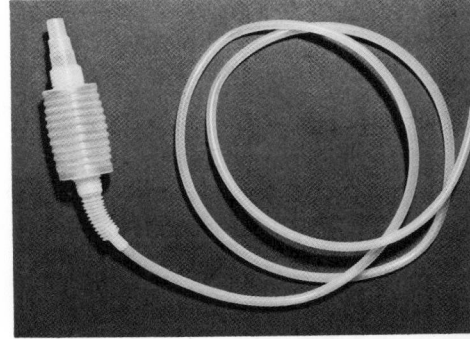

Tanks come in different sizes. They are measured by how much water they hold. One or two goldfish should have a five-and-a-half-gallon tank. So should a pair of guppies. They will look very small in the tank, but they will need all that room when they have babies. The tank is big enough for two dozen guppies. If you want to buy a fishbowl, get one that holds at least four gallons of water.

You will need a siphon for cleaning the tank. A siphon is a long plastic tube with a rubber squeeze bulb on it. Pages 20 to 21 tell how to use a siphon.

Buy a net, too. You will need a net whenever you have to move your fish to another container.

Fish food is sold in cans and boxes. Goldfish eat one kind of food. Guppies eat a different kind. The food comes in little grains or flakes. The brands that cost more are often better for your fish.

While you are in the store, you may see lots of other things you want—treasure chests and mermaids, machines that make bubbles, sparkly kinds of sand, and beautiful green plants. You can wait to get these things little by little. Your fish doesn't really need any of them, not even plants.

Buying a Fish

The photograph below shows the kinds of goldfish that are easiest to care for. The slim ones with the simple tails are called Comets. Some are gold, some are orange, some are black, and some are white. They come with spots and speckles of all these colors, too.

The black goldfish with pop eyes and a fancy tail is called a Moor. The fancy tail is called a fantail. Moors are short and plump.

The other plump fantailed goldfish is called a Fantail. Fantails come in all the colors that Comets come in. Their tails can grow longer and wavier than the tails of the Moors.

There are other even fancier goldfish. But they are harder to keep healthy than these three kinds. A goldfish that doesn't need very special care is better for a first fish.

It is hard to tell which goldfish are males, and which are females. Even if you are sure you chose a male and a female, they will not have babies. Goldfish don't usually lay their eggs in tanks.

Goldfish

Guppies

The guppies in the photograph are called Common Guppies. The smaller ones are the male fish. Their bodies are slim, and their tails are long. The males have beautiful colors on their bodies. You can see patches of bright green, blue, orange, and red. The bigger fish are the females. They have fat bellies in which they carry eggs. You can see through the skin on their bellies. The dark spot inside is the eggs they are carrying. The female guppies are not so colorful, but some have spots of color on their tails. Buy a male and a female guppy if you want your fish to have babies.

There are many kinds of guppies that are fancier than the Common Guppies. But they are not good for first fish. All of them need heaters in their tanks to keep them warm enough.

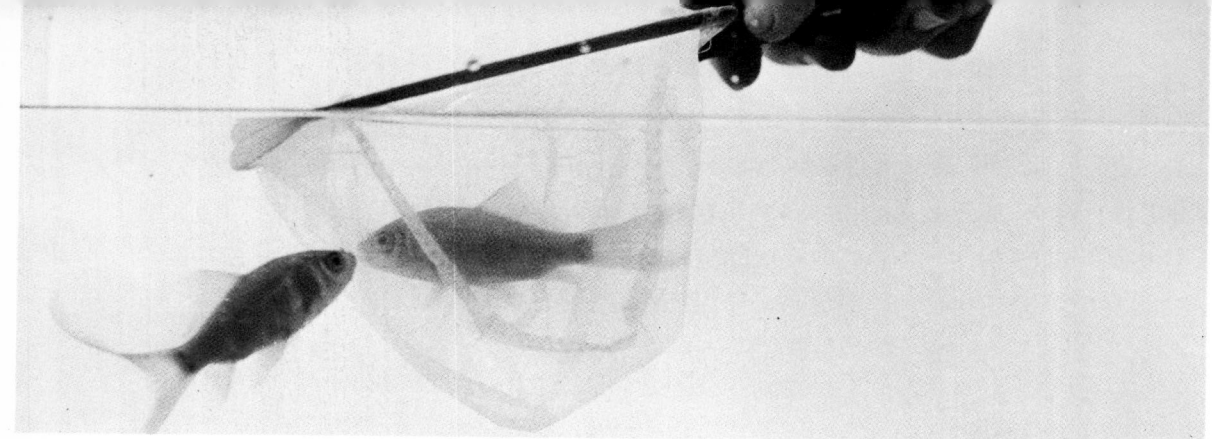

1

A New Fish

To move a fish to another container, net him from underneath (1), hold the net closed over the fish (2), turn the net upside down over the new container and release the fish (3). When you are buying a fish, he is then put into a plastic bag so you can carry him home (4, 5).

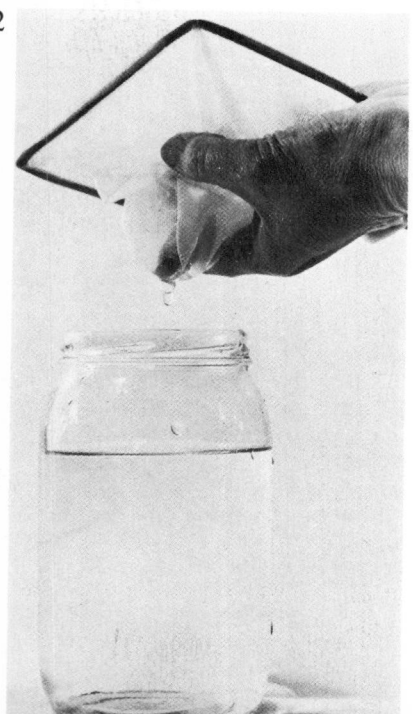

2

After you have chosen the tank and other equipment, you can pick out your fish. The pet store will have many fish all together in a big tank. Study them for a while. Look for a fish that is swimming a lot. If a fish isn't moving much, he may be sick. Look at the fins and tail. They shouldn't be nibbled or torn.

When you have chosen a fish, explain to the salesclerk which one you want. You can try pointing to him, but the fish may swim too fast for your finger to follow. So say what is special about him: he has a white belly or colorful speckles, or his tail is the longest of all.

The salesclerk will put her net in the tank and follow your fish with it. It can take her a few minutes to catch him gently. Watch how she nets the fish. You will have to do it yourself someday. The salesclerk moves the net slowly. She tries to get it under the fish. When the fish sees the net under him, he swims to the top. Then the salesclerk lifts up the net under his body. The fish is caught, and he has not bumped his head on the glass. The salesclerk holds the net closed over the fish. She turns it upside down over a jar of water. Then she opens her hand so the fish drops into the jar. Whenever you have to take your fish out of the tank, you can put him in a jar of water, too.

The salesclerk will pour the fish and the water into a plastic bag. She will tie the bag or close it with a rubber band so you can carry it home. When you get home, put the bag down on a table. The bag has enough air trapped inside to last the fish for an hour. He will be all right while you get his tank ready.

Wash out the tank with salt, just as you washed the pail. This time someone might have to help you. A tank is heavy and clumsy. Rinse it very well. Put the tank in a safe spot. (The next page tells you how to choose a good place for the tank.) Fill it with the water that you got ready earlier. Add drops of chlorine remover if you need to.

Now get the fish in his plastic bag. Put the bag in the tank of water. Let it float there for half an hour. The water in the bag will slowly get to exactly the same temperature as the water in the tank. The fish's body temperature will change slowly, too. Your fish won't get sick by suddenly getting warmer or cooler.

In half an hour, you can open the bag and let the fish swim out. If the top of the bag is held closed with a rubber band, take off the rubber band under the water. If the top of the bag is tied in a knot, cut off the top with scissors under water. The fish will swim out of the bag. Throw the bag away.

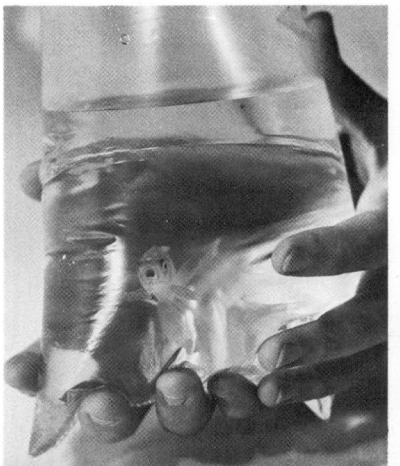

Where to Keep the Tank

You have to figure out the right place to keep the fish tank or bowl before you fill it with water. Tanks and bowls are very heavy and awkward to carry when they have water in them.

Keep your fish tank in a place that always stays at about the same temperature. The water in the tank can get cold too suddenly in a bedroom where windows are open on freezing nights. The water can heat up too fast in a sunny spot, or on a radiator, or underneath a lamp.

The kitchen counter is a good place for the tank. So is a shelf or table in the living room or family room. There should be an electric outlet nearby. You may need to plug in something for the tank later. Be sure you choose a spot where people and dogs won't bump into the tank. Don't put the tank in a room where you might play rough or throw balls. You could break the glass sides.

Goldfish stay healthiest in water that is at room temperature (65°-70°) or below. If the water slowly cools to 55° when the heat is turned down at night, the coolness will not harm them. The water might get as warm as 80° on a hot summer day. But the water warms up slowly, and the heat will not harm the fish.

Guppies do best in a room where their water does not get below 65°, even on cold nights. During the day, guppies need to be in water that is between 70° and 80°. If you live where the winters are very cold, or if your family likes a cool house, take the

temperature of the water with a regular outdoor thermometer. If the temperature of the water goes below 65° on cold nights, or below 70° during the daytime, you can move a lamp near the tank. The heat from a 60-watt bulb touching the side of the tank will warm the water enough.

Goldfish and guppies don't need much light. You can put them anywhere in a room except in hot sunlight. If you want plants growing in your tank, they may need special lighting. Page 39 explains about light for plants.

Chapter Two
Caring for Your Fish

Fish Food

Dried fish food is a mixture of dried vegetables and meats. The meats are usually shrimp and flies. The vegetables are usually potatoes and seaweed, and cereals such as bran and oatmeal. Goldfish food is mostly vegetables. Guppy food is mostly meat. Goldfish and guppies don't chew their food. They swallow pieces of food whole. If a piece is too big, they spit it out. If it is too small, they may not bother to eat it at all. So dried fish food comes in different sizes for different-sized fish. Goldfish food comes in bigger flakes or grains than guppy food. Baby guppy food is a powder. The giant goldfish on page 47 eats his food in pill-sized bits called pellets.

When you get tired of feeding your goldfish or guppy the same old dried food every day, you can give him surprise treats. Food that is alive is a special treat for fish. One kind of live food is brine shrimp.

Brine shrimp come two ways in pet stores. You can buy the eggs and hatch them yourself. Or you can buy the shrimp after they have hatched. Brine shrimp live in salt water. When you buy them hatched, the water they are swimming in is salty. Don't dump this salty water in your fish tank, because it would harm your fish. You have to catch some shrimp with your fishnet, and then put them in

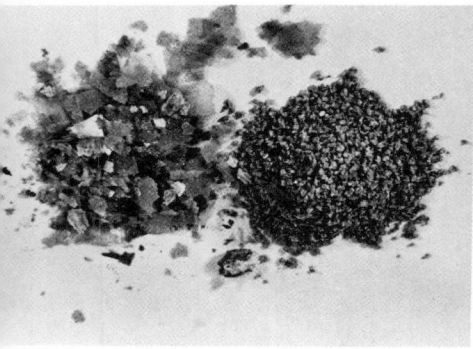
Dried fish food: flakes (left) and grains

Brine shrimp

your tank. If you buy eggs to hatch yourself, you put a few at a time in salt water. The directions on the package tell you how. The eggs hatch in a day. The shrimp can live for a week in the refrigerator. The rest of the eggs will last a long time if you keep them in a cool, dry place, such as on a shady window sill.

There are worms that goldfish and guppies will gobble up, too. Pet stores sell a worm called Tubifex. A goldfish can eat a Tubifex whole. A guppy can eat only small pieces of it. That means you have to cut it up. Earthworms (some people call them angleworms) are good treats, too. When you dig for earthworms in a garden, you may find baby ones only an inch long. A goldfish can eat them whole. If you find a big earthworm, it has to be cut up.

Just for a change you can try bits of lettuce leaves. Goldfish like to nibble them, and guppies might try them, too.

Guppies eat their food at the top of the water.

Feeding Your Fish

When you feed your fish, he will act enthusiastic. He notices when you sprinkle his food on the water. He swims up to get it and gobbles it greedily. He chases bits that fall from the top of the water. Feeding time seems to be a happy part of his day, and that makes you happy, too.

Because it is satisfying to feed a fish, people want to do it more and more. They give the fish too many meals. They give him too much food each time. This is how most pet fish get sick and die. They do not die because they eat too much. They die because they *don't* eat all the food. The extra food sinks down to the bottom of the tank. The fish eat some of it, but they can't eat it all. The leftover food rots. Germs grow in it. The germs use the air in the water for themselves. There is not enough air for the fish. And the germs make the fish sick, too.

This is the way to feed a fish so he eats everything you give him. Take a pinch of food out of the can or box. Put it in the palm of one hand. Then pick up just a few flakes and drop them into the water for your fish. Guppies eat the flakes at the top of the water. Goldfish eat the flakes on top and as they sink. Goldfish pick some of the food off the bottom, too. Watch your fish eat the first few flakes, and then give him a few more. Watch to see if he eats those, too. Feed him bit by bit this way until you can see he is not bothering to eat any more. He is full. That's all the food he wanted.

Now look in your hand. Is there still some food

left? If you had dumped it all in the water, that is how much would have been left over to rot in the bottom of the tank or bowl.

You can feed your fish twice a day, in the morning and in the evening. Or you can feed him only once, if that is easier. Put the food in the same corner of the tank every day. Your fish will learn where to come for his dinner. If some food does drop down to the bottom, he may learn where to find the leftovers.

There is a trick that you can teach a goldfish. First he has to get used to coming to the same corner of the tank for dinner. After a while, he will come there when he is hungry to see if any food is around. When he does, you know that he has learned the right spot. Now each time you feed him, first tickle the top of the water in the feeding corner. Your finger will make little ripples. The goldfish will feel the ripples with his body. Then feed your fish right away. Soon he will learn that your finger is calling him to dinner. He will swim right up to his dining room. You could say "Dinnertime!" too. The fish won't understand your words, but your friends will like the trick better.

19

Cleaning the Tank

People used to clean fish tanks just the way they washed dishes. They took the fish out, dumped out the dirty water, and scrubbed the tank with soap. Then they rinsed the tank and put in new water for their fish. The tank looked nice and clean, but many times the fish died.

Sometimes the soap wasn't completely rinsed out of the tank. Even tiny amounts of soap or detergent can kill a fish. Sometimes the new water was too warm or too cold. The fish couldn't live in it.

People don't wash tanks and bowls any more. Without removing the fish, they vacuum-clean the dirt off the bottom with a siphon. Siphoning is easier than washing. And the fish stay healthy.

A siphon is a plastic tube four or five feet long. You sweep one end of the tube along the bottom of the tank. It sucks up the wastes that make the tank dirty, just as a vacuum cleaner sucks up dirt from a rug. The other end of the tube goes into a pail on the floor. The dirty water empties into the pail.

You don't need a motor to make a siphon work. The water simply falls down through the tube. But the siphon won't work until the tube is full of water. The siphon comes with a rubber bulb on it. You squeeze the bulb to get water into the tube. The package that the siphon comes in tells how to do it.

When you siphon a tank, about a third of the water goes into the pail. You will need new water to take the place of the dirty water you throw away. Keep two or three gallons of water in plastic jugs. Keep them near your fish so they are the same temperature as the water in the tank. If your water has chlorine in it, add chlorine remover to each jug after you fill it. Put caps on the jugs to keep the water fresh.

A fish tank should be cleaned with a siphon once a week. The job takes about half an hour. Do it on a day when your family is not very busy. Siphoning is much easier if two people do it. One person sweeps the tank, and the other holds the bottom of the tube in the pail.

When it's time to clean the tank, get a pail for the dirty water. Get a chair to stand on if you cannot reach inside the tank. As soon as you get the siphon going, sweep it slowly back and forth across the floor of the tank. Don't forget the corners.

When the tank floor is clean, lift the siphon out of the tank. Let all the water in the tube empty into the pail. If you have baby guppies, check the pail to see if any are there. The siphon can easily suck up the tiny babies. Put them back into the tank with your net.

Pour the dirty water down the toilet or sink, and rinse the pail out. Then you can add new water to the tank from the plastic jugs. Fill up the jugs again so they are ready the next time you siphon the tank.

Self-Cleaning Tank

You don't have to use a siphon to clean your fish tank every week. A filter and a pump can do the job for you. This is what to buy if you want a self-cleaning tank: the smallest-size electric pump, a filter box that fits into a corner of the tank, three feet of plastic tubing, a bag of filter charcoal, and a bag of dacron filter fluff. You can buy everything in a pet store or pet department. Some places sell glass wool instead of dacron filter fluff. Glass wool works just as well, but many people are allergic to it. It makes them itch or sneeze.

To set up the filter, first rinse the charcoal in a strainer to wash away the charcoal dust. Read the directions that come with your filter to see how much charcoal to put in the box, and exactly where it goes. The filter fluff goes on top of the charcoal. The instructions say how much fluff to use, too.

When the box is filled with charcoal and fluff, attach the plastic tube to the top of the filter. Attach the other end of the tube to the pump. Lower the filter down into a corner of your tank. Plug in the pump. Some pumps start as soon as they are plugged in. Other pumps have a switch to turn them on.

When the pump is on, it sends bubbles of air up through the filter. Water is pulled through the filter, too. The charcoal and fluff trap any dirt in the water. The water comes out clean at the top of the filter. The bubbles are good for the fish, too, because they put more air in his water. You keep the pump running all the time except when you clean the filter.

The charcoal, the filter fluff, and the filter box

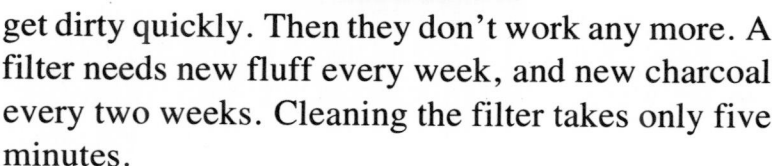

A self-cleaning fish tank. The pump could also sit below next to the tank. The filter box inside the tank shows black charcoal at the bottom and white filter fluff on top. Filters are not designed to fit into fishbowls.

get dirty quickly. Then they don't work any more. A filter needs new fluff every week, and new charcoal every two weeks. Cleaning the filter takes only five minutes.

Before you clean the filter, be sure to turn off the pump. The first week, throw out the used filter fluff and empty the charcoal into a strainer. Rinse it under running water in the sink. Wash the filter box with salt, not with soap. Rinse it well. Then put the charcoal back in the box, and add new fluff. The next week, throw out the dirty charcoal, too. Rinse the dust off some new charcoal and put it in the filter.

Even if you use a filter, you will have to siphon your tank three times a year. The filter does not trap quite all the dirt in the water. And your fish needs some fresh water now and then. Every four months, clean the bottom of the tank with a siphon. Take out a third of the water in the tank. Replace it with fresh water you have gotten ready the day before.

The water in a tank is always evaporating—slowly disappearing into the air. So keep a gallon of water ready in a plastic jug. Add some of it to the tank whenever you see the water is getting lower.

23

A Sick Fish

A clean tank helps to keep fish healthy. But even in a clean tank, fish can get sick. Fish sicknesses are hard to notice at first. By the time you see that a fish is sick, you may not be able to save him.

When a fish doesn't feel well, he may not be hungry. He swims slowly, or tips over on his side, or tilts his body head down. He may keep his fins folded, too. He stays down in the bottom of his tank, not moving around as much as he used to. Or he stays at the top, gulping for air. Sometimes you can see something wrong on his body. He may have tiny white spots or bigger white blisters, or his tail and fins may be ragged looking.

The first thing to do with a sick fish is to take him away from other fish. They could catch his sickness. Fill a jar with water from the tank. Catch the sick fish in your net the way the salesclerk did on page 12. Put him in the jar. That can be his hospital for now.

This may be the first time you have taken a fish from his tank and put him into a jar. What if you drop him? You may worry that your fish will die right away by breathing in air. A person would die by breathing in water. But a fish can keep alive in the air for a few minutes if he stays wet. If your fish falls or jumps from the net, just scoop him up gently and put him in the jar of water. The fish can stay in an open jar for a few hours.

You can make a larger hospital with a big mixing bowl. Fill it with the water that you keep in jugs for refilling the tank. Pour the sick fish out of the jar into the bowl. He will be more comfortable there.

Unless you can find someone who knows about fish sicknesses, there is not much hope for saving your fish. If you can, take your fish in his jar to the pet dealer. Or take him to a friend or neighbor who raises tropical fish. If they can tell what is wrong with your fish, they may know what to do or what medicine will help. But most of the time, a sick fish dies.

Fish die more easily than some other pets. It is not your fault. You tried to help. You will feel better if you give your dead fish a nice funeral. Wrap him in a pretty piece of cloth or in a fresh green leaf. Bury him in the ground, or in the bottom of a flower pot. His body will make plants grow better. You could plant a flower on his grave.

Chapter Three
Fish Watching

Fish Bodies

You can spend a lot of time watching fish. There's a surprising amount to see and learn. People who are interested in fish have found out many things about them just by watching. They have learned other things by doing experiments. They have looked carefully at a fish's body to understand the way it works.

A fish has gills on both sides of his head, where you have cheeks. A fish flaps his gills open and shut all the time. He opens and closes his mouth all the time, too. He is breathing. He takes a gulp of water. His mouth pushes the water into his gills. Air is dissolved in the water. The gills take the air out of it. Then they flap to push the water out of the fish's body.

Some fish can breathe air from above the water. Guppies can't, but goldfish can. If they do not get enough air from their water, goldfish go to the top of the tank. They gulp a bubble of air. They push it through their gills. If your goldfish gulps air often his tank may be too small. Or germs in rotting food may be using up all the air in the water.

Fish gulp with their mouths to eat as well as to breathe. Goldfish and guppies don't have teeth. The bones around their mouths are hard enough to use for biting. You may see your fish bite off a piece of lettuce to eat. He will swallow it whole. Fish can spit things out, too. Watch a fish in a tank with sand at the bottom. When he gulps a bit of food off the bottom, he may gulp a mouthful of sand along with it. He spits the sand right out.

If you look at a fish's mouth, you can tell where in the water he eats most of his food. Fish that find most of their food at the top, as guppies do, have mouths that point upward. Fish that eat from the bottom have mouths that point downward. Goldfish eat a lot of their food between the top and the bottom. Their mouths point straight ahead.

Instead of arms and legs, a fish has little side fins. The fins are always moving. A fish stretches out his side fins to help him stop. He moves them in different ways to help him turn. The fish moves his side fins to keep himself balanced, too. Try walking on a narrow board. You hold your arms out and move them to help you keep your balance. When a fish swims, he uses his side fins in the same way.

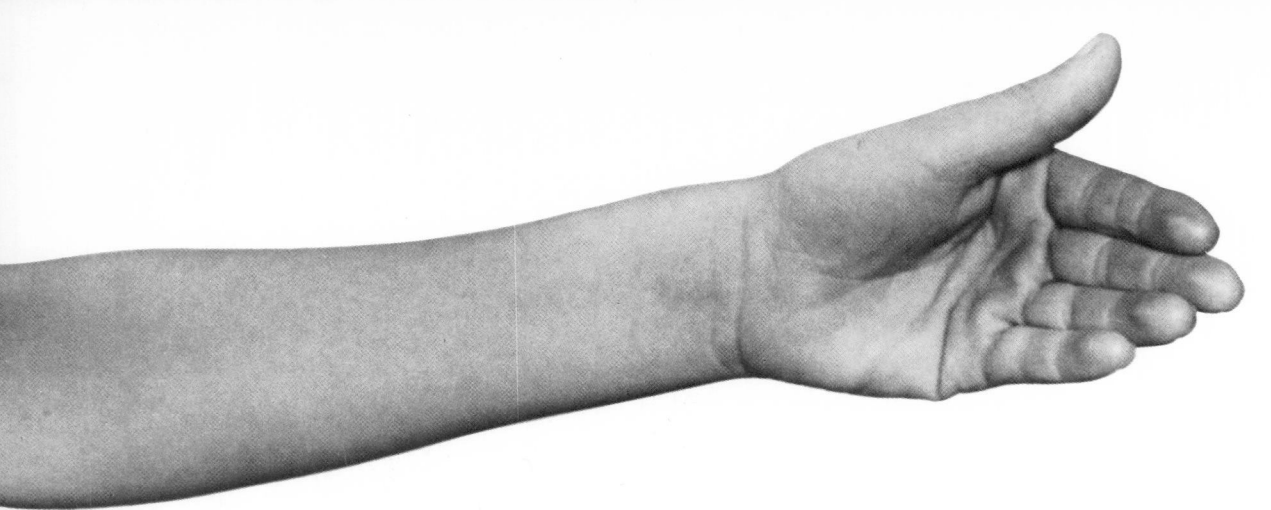

A fish's top and bottom fins help to hold his body straight. When a fish is resting, he stretches out his top and bottom fins as far as they will go. They keep him steady. When a fish wants to go fast, he folds his top and bottom fins close to his body. Then his body is streamlined like a racing car. He can swim much faster. You can see your fish fold his fins when he swims fast.

The shape of a fish is perfect for moving through water. Water is easy to cut through. When you take a bath, pretend your hand is a fish. Hold your hand flat, and move it straight ahead. The tips of your fingers, like the nose of a fish, cut easily through the water. Now wiggle your hand from side to side. The flat sides of your hand, like the flat sides of a fish's body, push against the water. A fish pushes his body from side to side to make himself move forward. He swings his tail from side to side, too.

Watch your fish's tail when he turns. His tail steers him. When he turns his tail one way, his head goes the other way. A rudder on a sailboat works the

same way. But a fish moves his tail so quickly, you have to look sharp to see how he turns.

Fish don't swim all the time. Sometimes they stop and rest, or they go to sleep. You can't be sure if your fish is resting or is really asleep because fish have no eyelids. Their eyes are always open. And goldfish and guppies don't lie down on their sides to sleep. But if you see your fish staying quite still near the bottom of the tank at night, he is most likely asleep.

When you look closely at a fish, you can see that his body is covered with scales. The skin underneath the scales is thin and tender. It could be easily torn. The scales protect the fish's skin. The scales are hard, but you can see through them just as you can see through your fingernails. You can see the beautiful colors of the fish's skin.

A fish has a slippery body. Water and plants slide over it easily. Enemies have trouble holding onto it. If you have ever tried to catch a fish in your hands, you know how his slippery body helps him escape.

Fish Senses

Even though fish live in water, they can see, hear, smell, taste, and touch. You can see that your fish has eyes. When you are watching your fish, is he watching you? He might be. He can see through the glass. But your face looks blurry to him. He is quite nearsighted. Fish have no eyelids because they don't need them. They don't need to blink. The water they live in keeps their eyes wet and clean.

You can do an experiment to find out if your fish has favorite colors. Turn off the lights at night. Shine a green Christmas-tree light or a flashlight covered with blue cellophane into one corner of your fish's tank. He might swim into the colored light. Try other colors. Some fish don't seem to notice red.

Fish have ears inside their bodies. You cannot see them, but the fish can hear. Fish can talk to one another, too. They don't talk with words as people

do. Instead, they make special noises to say hello to other fish, or to tell other fish to swim along with them. You won't be able to hear your goldfish or guppies talk. The sounds they make are too faint.

A fish has two nostrils. He doesn't breathe through them, but he can smell very well with them. He can smell his dinner in the water.

Your tongue has taste buds on it that tell you when food is salty, or sour, or sweet, or bitter. Fish have taste buds, too. But a fish's taste buds are not all in his mouth. Many are on his body. A fish can taste with the skin under his scales. He can taste his food before it is even in his mouth.

A fish can feel with his skin, too. Your fish could feel you touching him. If someone touches you too hard, it hurts. But people are not sure a fish can feel pain. When a fish gets a hook caught in his mouth, he swims about as though nothing had happened. The hook doesn't seem to hurt him.

Fish find out things about their world another way, too. They have a "sixth" sense, a sense that people don't have. Look at your fish. On each side of his body, there is a line running along the middle. Under that line is a canal filled with liquid. Other smaller canals spread out from it. When anything makes the water move, the liquid in the canals moves, too. The fish can tell where the movement is coming from. Water moves around a rock in a certain way. If there is a rock in the water, the fish knows where it is. He doesn't bump into it, even at night. He can feel another fish coming toward him. He can feel an insect hit the top of the water. He can feel your finger tickle the water at dinnertime, too.

Fish Babies

Guppy families are fun to watch. If you buy a male and a female guppy, they will surely mate and have babies. They will have babies in one month. They will keep on having babies every month all year long. Twenty or even fifty babies will be born every month.

When the male guppy is ready to mate, he follows the female. He catches up to her and then swims in front. He shakes his body so the female will notice him. He swims backwards toward her, so she will see the bright colors on his tail. If the female likes all this showing off, she mates with the male guppy. She lets him put a fluid called sperm inside her body. She has eggs in her body that need sperm in order to grow.

If you look very closely at the male, you will see a long, pale tube that hangs down between his back fins. The tube is called a gonopodium. The male's sperm comes through the gonopodium to the female's eggs.

Most female fish lay their eggs in the water before the male puts his sperm on them. Then the fish swim away and forget about the eggs. But a female guppy keeps her eggs in her body until they grow into babies. You can see the dark eggs through the skin of the mother's belly. You can see her belly grow bigger as the babies grow. Look carefully. You may be able to see the babies' eyes.

When it is time for the babies to be born, the female goes down to the bottom of the tank. She finds a private place. Then she begins to shake her body. Out pops a baby, curled up inside a thin bubble. He wiggles to break the bubble, then he swims away fast. His mother shakes some more. Each time she shakes another baby is born. The baby fish are called "fry." That's where the expression "small fry" comes from.

You would think that when a mother has kept her eggs in her belly for a month, she would take care of the fry after they are born. But mother and father guppies do not act like parents. They do not even know that the fry are their babies. Sometimes they just ignore them. Sometimes they think the fry are food. They chase them and try to eat them.

The fry don't know that they have a mother and a father. They think all bigger fish are enemies. They swim away and hide. Plants make good places for baby guppies to hide. (Pages 38 to 39 tell you about plants that you can grow in your tank.)

Feed brine shrimp that have just hatched to guppy fry. Newly hatched brine shrimp are small enough for baby guppies to eat. Feed them dry food, too. The dry food for baby guppies is a powder. Feed the fry three times a day at first. When the babies begin to taste flakes of their parents' food, you can stop feeding them baby food.

Baby guppies grow quickly. In two or three months they are grown up enough to have babies of their own. Their mother and father are still having babies, and now they can have babies, too. The tank they live in does not grow. Soon it is too small for so many fish.

33

You don't have to do anything about a crowded tank if you don't want to. As the tank gets crowded, it will be like life in the wild. Bigger fish will eat smaller fish. Stronger fish will live. Weaker fish will die. Grownups will have fewer babies, and smaller ones. After a while, your tank will be like a tiny wild world. There will always be some grownups, and there will always be some babies. But many babies will die when they are tiny, just as they do in the wild.

If you feel that letting baby fish die is mean, there are other things you can do. But they are harder.

You can buy only male guppies. Then there won't be any babies. But that is not so much fun. You can buy a male and a female but let them live together for only a month or so. Then move the male to another tank. The female will probably have babies four times after the male is gone. But then she will stop. You will have lots of babies to watch.

Before these babies grow up—before they are two months old—you can give them to friends. Or when they are almost two months old, you can put all the boys in with the father guppy, and leave all the girls in with the mother guppy. Sorting out the babies is a lot of work. And it is not always easy to tell the boys from the girls. Boy guppies are a bit smaller than girl guppies. And the boys have a little more color. But sometimes it's hard to see any difference.

Here is how to sort the babies. Fill two jars with water from the mother's tank. Scoop up two or three babies at a time with your net. Pick up ones you think are boys and put them in one jar. Pick up ones you think are girls and put them in the other jar. Don't pick up the fish between your fingers. Put your fingers under each fish and lift it into the jar. Pour the jar of boys into the father's tank, and the jar of girls into the mother's tank.

Chapter Four
Underwater Worlds

After a while, you may get tired of watching your fish swim about in a plain tank. Maybe your fish is tired of a plain tank, too. He has no place to explore and no place to hide. He has nothing new to look at either.

It is time to make an underwater world. Think how you would like the world to be if you lived underwater. It could be green and waving with grass. The ground could be a bright color. There could be a cave.

Gravel for Your Tank

The first thing you need is sand or gravel for the bottom of the tank. Pet stores sell kinds of sand and gravel that are safe for fish. Eight pounds are enough for a five-and-a-half-gallon tank. That will give you about two inches of ground.

Sand and gravel come plain and in bright colors. If you use a plain kind, your tank will look like the natural bottom of a pond or stream. Colored sand or gravel turns the tank into a make-believe world.

One kind of sand has very tiny grains. It is called terrarium sand. Buy it only if you have a filter in your tank. A siphon sucks up too much of it.

Gravel is rougher looking than sand. One kind of gravel, called glass gravel, is made of crushed glass instead of crushed rock. It has the brightest colors and sparkles like jewels. You can put glass gravel in a guppy tank, but don't use it with goldfish. They can cut their mouths on it when they eat food from the bottom.

Before you use the sand or gravel you have to rinse it well with plain water. Pour it into a pail or big bowl. Slowly run lukewarm water into the pail and let it overflow. Stir up the sand or gravel while the water is overflowing. When the water looks clean, turn off the tap and ask someone to help you pour the water off the gravel. Now it will be clean enough to use. (Page 42 tells you how to add the sand or gravel to your tank.)

Left to right: coarse gravel, glass gravel, and two shades of terrarium sand

Plants for Your Tank

All the plants in these pictures are easy to grow in a fish tank. They can put their roots in sand or gravel. They do not need heated water.

The first three plants are sold as bunches of stems. The stems grow roots after you plant them. The other three are sold as whole plants with roots. These six plants are all common and can be bought in most pet stores. Two or three plants are plenty for a five-and-a-half-gallon tank. (Directions for planting them are on pages 42 to 43.)

The bunched stems are often sold with a plant weight holding each bunch together. The weight is a flat wire made of soft lead. It keeps the stems from floating all over the tank. Some bunches are sold with a rubber band around them. You have to buy separate plant weights for those. Rubber bands are so tight that they keep the stems from growing.

Anacharis (or Elodea) is a plant that goldfish love to eat. Some people keep a bunch of Anacharis stems until the leaves are eaten up. Then they buy a new bunch.

Creeping Charlie stems grow roots quickly. The stems quickly grow taller, too. Soon the plants grow right out of the top of your tank.

Cabomba stems grow roots slowly. Cabomba is feathery and tangled. Baby guppies especially like to hide among its stems. Cabomba has white flowers that open like bells under the water.

Top to bottom: Anacharis, Creeping Charlie, Cabomba

Corkscrew Vallisneria has grassy leaves that twist around like corkscrews. They wave about when the fish swim by.

Brazilian Sword Plant has big dark leaves. It grows fast and becomes quite large.

Banana Plants float. Little "balloons" keep the plant floating. The balloons look like bunches of bananas. Roots grow down from the plant and sometimes reach all the way to the gravel. But Banana Plants are supposed to float, so don't try to plant them at the bottom.

All these plants need light to grow. A bright room, where you can read a book without turning a lamp on, may have enough light. Wait a month and see if your plants grow. If they don't, they need more light. You can buy a light fixture that is especially made to fit the top of your tank. Ask for the fixture that holds a Gro-Lux bulb. The Gro-Lux is made especially for plants. Keep it on for four to six hours a day to give the plants enough light.

Sometimes a tank gets too much light. The water looks green or brown. The glass sides get green and fuzzy. The fuzz is tiny plants called algae. Algae won't hurt your fish. Fish eat algae and it is good food for them. But if you don't like your tank full of green fuzz, here is what to do: Don't keep the Gro-Lux bulb on for so long. Or try to shade the tank with a piece of cardboard or some potted plants. Or move the tank to a darker part of the room. Or buy a snail. He will eat up the algae.

Top to bottom: Corkscrew Vallisneria, Brazilian Sword Plant, Banana Plant

Decorations for Your Tank

Do you want some rocks or a cave in your tank? You have to be careful about the rocks you use. Many kinds of rock are not safe. They have minerals and metals in them that can dissolve in water. The minerals and metals could harm your fish. Slate is a safe rock. So is quartz, and so is granite. These and other safe rocks are sold in pet stores. If you find a pretty rock yourself, but can't find out if it is safe, don't use it. Rinse any rocks or pebbles very well before you put them in your tank. Don't use shells and corals. Shells and corals both have lime in them. Lime is bad for fish.

Rocks for a fish tank

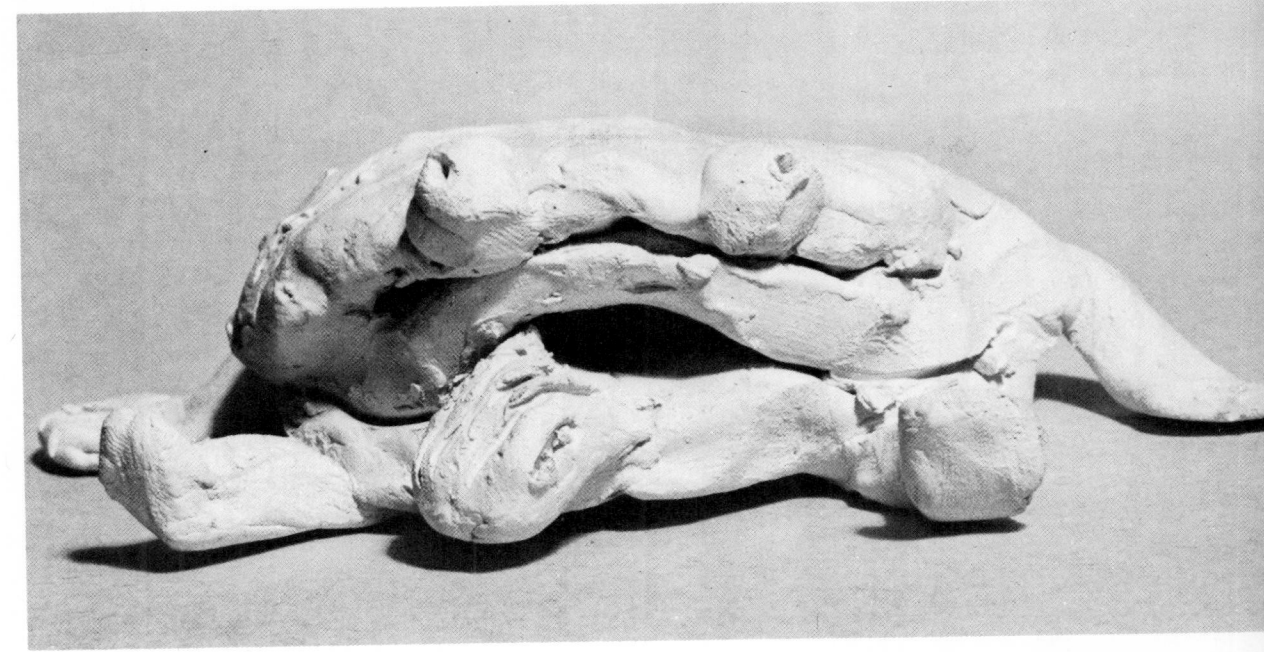

Anything that is made of smooth glass or china is safe to put in your tank. You can use little china animals or smooth lumps of glass or marbles. If your school or a friend has a kiln for baking clay, you can make clay bridges or caves or castles or anything you like. Use boneware clay or terra cotta pottery clay. Bake your clay decorations in the kiln. Glaze them, too, if you want. The baked clay and the glazes are both safe. But you can't use decorations made of plaster, because plaster has lime in it. And you can't use self-hardening clays or the kinds you bake in the kitchen oven, because they will dissolve in water.

Plastic things are safe for fish, too. Some stores sell plastic bubbles. A plastic duck could float on top of the water.

A homemade monster of baked clay to decorate an underwater world

41

Setting Up Your Underwater World

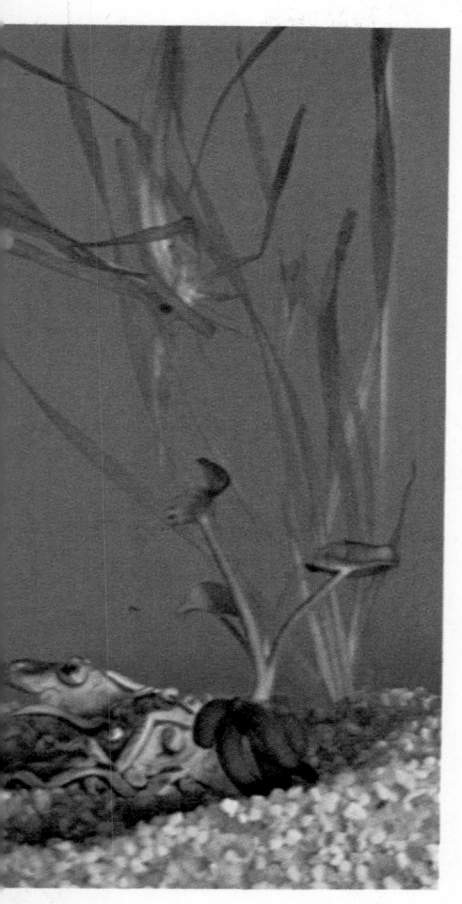

When you have clean sand or gravel, plants, and safe rocks, you can make your fish his new world. Or you can add just gravel one week, and a plant another time, and a rock later on.

Before you add anything, fill a jar with water from your fish's tank. Catch your fish in his net and put him in the jar. If you don't have a filter, siphon the bottom of the tank to clean it. But don't replace any water yet. If you do have a filter, take some water out of the tank and save it. You don't want the tank to overflow when you work in it.

Put the washed sand or gravel in the tank first. Scoop it in with a large spoon or a plastic bowl. Push it around with your hands. Make hills with it if you like hills. Or make the sand high in the back and low in the front of the tank. Leftover food and dirt will fall down to the front. Then the tank will be easier to clean. A little sand will get sucked up when you siphon. But less sand will be lost if you only have to siphon the front.

Plant Corkscrew Vallisneria and Brazilian Sword Plant next. Gently stick the roots down into the sand or gravel. Make a little hill around each plant to hold it. Plants that have small roots won't stay in the sand or gravel well. Pile some small stones around them to hold their roots in place.

Next, put rocks where you want them. Two rocks with a flat rock across the top will make a bridge. If it is big enough, your fish will swim through it. You could build a cave in a corner for a hiding place. You could put little stones into the ground to make a path. You could build a wall.

When the rocks are where you want them, put in the plants that come in bunches. If a bunch has a rubber band around it instead of a plant weight, cut the stems above the rubber band. Throw away the bottom part. Loosely twist a plant weight around the remaining stems, near the lower end.

You have to plant each bunch under a rock to hold it down. First bury the stem bottoms sideways in the gravel or sand. Stick them in far enough to hide the plant weight. Then put a rock over the buried stem bottoms. In time, they will grow roots in the ground.

Now put in anything else you want, such as china animals or glass jewels. When you've made your underwater world just the way you want it, you can put floating plants such as Banana Plants on top. They would have gotten in your way before. Check the water level in the tank. If it is low, put some water back in.

When you put your fish into his new world, he may act surprised. Maybe he will swim about very fast. He may not want to explore yet. Be patient with him. You might feel worried, too, if everything around you were suddenly different. In a few hours your fish will feel comfortable. Then he can be interested in the things you have given him.

You may want to change your fish's world later, or add something new. Put your fish in a jar of water from the tank first. He would be scared to see your hands inside his tank. He might swim away too fast and bump himself on the glass.

Fish Company

You might wonder if your fish gets lonely. Goldfish and guppies don't seem to mind living alone. But you could get another fish to keep your fish company. Or you could bring other creatures to visit your fish in his world.

Some other animals can live in the tank all the time. A snail can live there. Snails are good housekeepers because they eat the green algae that grows in tanks. But snails may eat the other plants, too, so one snail is enough.

Snail

A crayfish can live with your fish. Crayfish look like small lobsters. A pet store can order one for you. Or you might find one living in a stream or pond. Crayfish eat food that falls to the bottom of the tank. So they are good housekeepers, too.

A newt or a tadpole could visit your fish. You might find a newt swimming in a pond. Drop some crumbs of bread into the water. See if a newt comes to eat. Catch it with your fishnet. A newt eats what the fish eats. But after a few days it should go back to its own pond.

Crayfish

You might find a tadpole in the pond, or a bunch of frog's eggs in their jelly. Catch a tadpole, or take two or three eggs from the bunch. Watch the eggs become tadpoles, and the tadpoles become frogs. Tadpoles will eat fish food and algae. But when they become frogs, they need to catch live insects for food. Take them back to their own pond then.

44

You might find insects called water striders and whirligig beetles on a pond. They rush about on top of the water. They are very hard to catch. If you get one in your net, it could live in your tank for a while. Both of these insects are too big for your fish to eat, and too fast for him to catch.

If you have a pet turtle, he can visit the fish tank for a swim. But watch him. He might nibble on your fish's tail. If he chases the fish, you have to take him out. If he behaves nicely, let him stay a little longer. Float a piece of wood on the water so he can climb out and rest.

Newt

Tadpole

Water strider

Turtle

Giant Goldfish

It's fun to raise small fish in a small underwater world. But you can also raise a giant fish to live in a big world.

The fish in this picture is a giant goldfish. When he is hungry, he swims back and forth very fast until you notice him. When you walk towards his tank, he swims to the top. He puts his mouth up out of the water. When you feed him, he snatches the food right out of your fingers.

This giant is not a special kind of goldfish. He was once a small goldfish in a small tank. But he has had a special life. Now he lives in a big tank.

Here is how to raise a giant goldfish. Let your little goldfish live alone in his five-and-a-half-gallon tank. He will have lots of space to swim in. Use a filter. The bubbles will give him lots of air to breathe. Feed him dried food, and also feed him live food such as brine shrimp a few times a week. He will have a good appetite.

When your goldfish has grown to three or four inches long, move him to an 18-gallon tank. Buy a *high* tank, not a *long* tank. A goldfish gets more exercise in a high tank. You can decorate this tank just as you decorated the small one.

At first your fish looks silly in his new tank. He is a small fish in a giant world. But he grows. You begin to feed him a new kind of food. Flakes are too small for him. He needs pill-sized pellets of food. He grows some more. He can eat big worms. And he still grows more. One day he is not silly any more. He is a giant fish in his giant world.

46

Index